Galatians

Born (again!) to Be Free

Linda Osborne

Published by Catch the Vision! Press

504 A Harbor View Drive, Klamath Falls, OR 97601

ISBN-10: 0615803938
ISBN-13: 978-0615803937

DEDICATION

To my wonderful mother, Carol, who has always loved me unconditionally and given me room to be who I am, which is such an important aspect of freedom!

CONTENTS

A WORD FROM THE AUTHOR

If there has been one thing I have struggled with in my Christian walk, it has been the struggle to be free. Yes, I know that in Christ I am free. That is a done deal. I know that clearly in my mind. In fact, I have endeavored to teach that concept each and every time I have had the opportunity. On a personal level, though, it has been elusive for me. I know it and I believe it, yet it has been hard for me to turn from head knowledge into heart knowledge.

Although we know that our enemy doesn't have the ability to read our thoughts, he does seem to have a way to find our areas of weakness. I believe this is part of the problem for me. He has noticed my weakness in this area of living free. He has seen my tendency to be legalistic; to try to earn my Savior's love and acceptance. He has used this weakness to his advantage and to my disadvantage. But praise be to God, greater is He who is in me than he who is in the world (1 John 4:4)! Though the lies of the enemy are strong, the truth of the Lord is stronger and will certainly prevail!

I am discovering daily the freedom to love and be loved, to accept that I am accepted, and to receive apart from giving. It is my hope to share this freedom with you as together we study this wonderful letter to the church in Galatia. Open your heart to the deep truths that this letter holds. May you come out of this study freer than you went in!

GETTING STARTED

It is always good to begin a study by looking at the book as a whole. You may, therefore, want to read this entire letter in one sitting before you get started with your verse by verse study. It would also be helpful to your study of Galatians to read the first eight chapters of Paul's letter to the Romans.

Your lesson will be divided into five-day increments. Each day you will be given a chapter of Scripture to read and then you will be asked questions based on that passage and others relating to it. The questions will range from the *facts* of the passage to *personal application* and, finally, to questions that will encourage you to *dig a little deeper* on your own. Each lesson will have a *Stone of Remembrance*—a verse which is applicable to the lesson at hand—for you to commit to memory. Finally, you will be able to pull it all together in an overview of the passage you have been studying all week. As much as is possible, try to do your lesson on a daily basis. And, always remember to pray before you begin your study each day, asking the Holy Spirit to speak to you in a personal way.

PREFACE

On the day Paul sat down to write this letter, he knew what he had to say was of the utmost importance. The church in Galatia was headed in the wrong direction; they had taken a wrong turn. Leaving a relationship of grace, they were headed straight into a religion of legalism. Although there were Jews in Galatia, the Galatians were Gentiles. They hadn't grown up governed by the Jewish law. They may have known little about the religious system of the Jews. When it came to the rites and rituals of Judaism, they were like blank slates. Then Paul brought them the good news of Jesus Christ. The God of the universe spoke to them through His servant Paul, and they were brought into a relationship with Him through the work of His Son. But a corrupting influence soon set in. By way of false teachers, they were introduced to a new perspective on what Paul had taught them, and they listened. Their heads were turned. They didn't realize they were listening to a lie. Paul had to set them straight with the truth.

What Paul couldn't have known was the importance this letter would have to the Church as a whole through the years. The letter to the Galatians has been cited as being the cornerstone of the Reformation. It has been called the Magna Carta of spiritual liberty, the Christian's declaration of independence. It was the backbone of Martin Luther's cry, as he learned from this great epistle, along with Paul's letter to the Romans, that salvation is by faith alone—a message which he proclaimed to all who would listen, at great personal cost.

How important is this letter to us today? As important as it ever was! Who hasn't struggled with the notion that they must work for their salvation? How many churches in our day put forth a message that you must do "certain things" in order to know that you are truly saved? Whether you are encouraged by a church, by your own weakness, or by the devil himself to work for your salvation, it is time that you know it is a lie and not the true gospel message. Martin Luther was a troubled and tormented soul who never thought he could do enough to please God. But he found rest for his soul from the teachings of this letter—and you can too!

The theme for this study will be *Freedom in Christ.* And the key verse, Galatians 5:1, *"Stand fast therefore in the liberty by which Christ has made us free, and do not be entangled again with a yoke of bondage."*

LESSON ONE
Galatians 1

Day 1
Daily Facts

Read Galatians 1 as a whole, and then reread verses 1-5 for today's study.

1. Who wrote this letter? v. 1

   ✣ Who does he include in his greeting? v. 2

   ✣ To whom is this letter written?

2. Paul immediately identifies his position in this letter as an apostle. In what way does he *qualify* his position? v. 1

   ✣ Why do you think he might have presented himself in this way?

   ✣ Share several truths about Jesus Christ as presented by Paul in the very first verses of his letter to the Galatians.

3. What word of personal greeting does Paul give the Galatians? v. 3

It has been noted that Galatians is the only epistle in which Paul gives no word of commendation to its readers.

- ✢ Considering the brief opening of Paul's letter and the words he immediately moves on to in verse 6, what do you sense is the state of Paul's heart/mind as he sits to write to the Galatians?

Making it Personal

4. How do you respond when you see someone you love begin to follow *a different gospel* (verse 6)? Do you ignore it and hope it will go away? Do you stop associating with them and only talk to your *right-on* Christian friends? Do you pray for them? Do you rush in and remind them of the truth? Is this an area you need to work on? Share your thoughts.

    - ✢ How can we know what is true?

Digging Deeper

- ✢ Using the introduction to Galatians in your Bible or a Bible dictionary, share a little background on Galatia. You may also want to look for Galatia on your Bible map.

- ✢ Do your best to summarize today's passage in a couple of sentences.

Stone of Remembrance: "And you shall know the truth, and the truth shall make you free." John 8:32

Day 2

Daily Facts

Read Galatians 1:6-10

In Acts, we learn that Paul came to Galatia on his first missionary journey, along with Barnabas, between A.D. 46 and 48. There he established churches in Antioch, Iconium, Lystra, and Derbe. Although there are several theories as to the date of this letter, it is possible that it was written between his first missionary journey and his second missionary journey (which began in A.D. 49). If this were the case, Galatians would be Paul's first epistle and one of the earliest documents of the New Testament. It would also mean that not much time had passed since he had been in their presence.

1. Why was Paul so amazed, according to verse 6?

Look at verses 6-7 in the NASB: "I am amazed that you are so quickly deserting Him who called you by the grace of Christ, for a different gospel; which is really not another; only there are some who are disturbing you, and want to distort the gospel of Christ."

2. According to these verses:

   - What have the false teachers caused the Galatians to do with Christ?

   - What are the Galatians turning to?

   - What are the false teachers doing to the Galatians?

   - What have they done with the true gospel message?

3. How emphatically did Paul make the point that no one had the right to change the message he had already preached to the Galatians? vv. 8-9

- What did Paul mean when he said the words "let him be accursed"?

- Was Paul a man pleaser? What was he?

Making it Personal

We know that the Bible can be taught by different people, from different angles, and with a different emphasis, without changing the truth. But if any of the truth is changed, then it becomes a false teaching. The dangerous thing about false teaching is that it is often predominantly true, but with one important and dangerous lie thrown in.

4. On a scale of 1-10 (10 being the best):

   - How well do you know your Bible?

   - Would you be able to detect a small lie being mixed in with the truth?

5. From the standpoint of 2 Timothy 2:15, and what we are studying today, why is it important that you study your Bible?

   - Considering our memory verse, why do you think knowing the truth makes you free?

Digging Deeper

Acts 13-14 records Paul's first missionary journey, in which he founded the churches of Galatia. Look at Acts 13:14-14:23 and make note of any interesting things you discover about his mission to the Galatians. Notice in particular the work of the Judaizers against the ministry of Paul. These are most likely the very ones who were bothering the Galatians at the time of this letter.

- Do your best to summarize today's passage in a couple of sentences.

- Review your memory verse.

Day 3

Daily Facts

Read Galatians 1:11-24 (we'll be concentrating on verses 11-18 today)

The attack was not only on the true gospel message but, in order to make a case, the false teachers had to also attack the one who brought it—Paul. In this passage, which we will study today and tomorrow, Paul will defend his ministry.

1. How did Paul begin this very letter defending his apostleship? See verse 1.

    - See if you can explain why it was important that Paul's ministry come from Christ and not from men.

It was not only important that the Galatians knew that Paul was a true apostle, chosen by God Himself for this role, but that the message he had given them had not been given to him by man but by God.

2. Share the declaration made by Paul on this important point in verses 11-12.

    - Paul made a case for this fact by sharing his history before and after he met Christ. Look at verses 13-18, and share the points of Paul's testimony that make the case that Paul received his message from God and not from man.

Making it Personal

Paul makes his calling by God very personal in verses 15-16, when he says that he was set apart from his mother's womb and called by God's grace to preach the gospel to the Gentiles. Paul recognized that he didn't choose God, God chose him! Have you discovered this truth yet?

3. Look at the testimony of a king and a prophet on this same point and share what you learn from them:

   - *Psalm 139:13-16*

   - *Jeremiah 1:4-5*

4. Paul saw that he was called not only to be saved, but also to serve. How does Jesus speak this same word to you, His disciple? John 15:16

5. How do these verses minister to you personally?

Digging Deeper

- Paul was the only apostle who needed to defend his ministry. He had not been one of the original 12. He was not the one chosen to replace Judas, after he betrayed Jesus. He came after. One of the requirements of apostleship was seeing the resurrected Christ, as the apostles were the "ones sent out" to witness to His Resurrection. Look at 1 Corinthians 15:7-10a and share Paul's own testimony to having seen the risen Christ—a proof of the legitimacy of his ministry.

- Do your best to summarize today's passage in a couple of sentences. (Specifically verses 11-18.)

- Review your memory verse.

Day 4

Daily Facts

Read Galatians 1:11-24

Today we will continue to study Paul's defense of his ministry and his message. To get the best understanding we can of the timeline of events, we will look at all the verses in our passage today.

1. Again, what is the point of this passage from Paul's point of view? vv. 11-12

2. Using each verse in this passage, let's make our own timeline of Paul's history. Share specifically what each verse tells us about Paul.

   - Pre-conversion

     verse 13

     verse 14

   - Conversion

     verse 15-16a

- Post-conversion

  verse 16b

  verse 17

  verse 18-19

  verse 21

- If we look ahead to Galatians 2:1, we will get the last step in the timeline Paul has created. What does it tell us?

3. What other points does Paul make to emphasize the fact that he got his message straight from Christ and not from men?

   verse 20

   verse 22

- What was the reaction of those who were hearing of the conversion of Paul the persecutor? vv. 23-24

Making it Personal

4. In our lesson this week, we have been considering the testimony of Paul. If you are a Christian, you have a testimony too! Although Paul would have a lot more to say about what happened at the time of his conversion, in Galatians he shared only a few key things. Why don't you follow Paul's example here and write a statement of a few sentences describing your conversion, including a word about your *pre-conversion, conversion,* and *post-conversion* experience?

Digging Deeper

- Yesterday we considered Paul's testimony to having seen the risen Christ. Today we will look at his actual experience. Paul shares different aspects of his experience in Acts 9:1-19, Acts 22 3-15, and Acts 26:12-18. Choose at least one of these passages and share what you learn about Paul's conversion.

- Do your best to summarize today's passage in a couple of sentences.

- Review your memory verse.

Day 5

Overview of Galatians 1

Today we will be looking at the passage we have studied this week as a whole. The goal is to find the main lessons the Lord has for us from this chapter. Don't worry about being clever or profound—just do your best!

Find the Facts ...

1. See if you can state the *content* of this week's passage in a couple of sentences. You can use your daily summary statements to help you come up with one main theme or summary of the chapter. (Who is speaking, what is taking place, what is the main subject?)

Look for the Heart ...

2. What do you think is the main *lesson* of this chapter? (What spiritual truths are taught here? Look for a command, a word of exhortation, a promise, etc.)

Hear Him Speak ...

3. Look for a *personal application* from the content of this chapter. It should come from the lesson you got from the chapter (question 2). How will you apply the lesson to yourself?

4. Was there a particular verse that ministered to you this week? What was it and how did it minister to you?

5. Write out your stone of remembrance *from memory.*

LESSON TWO
Galatians 2

We begin our study of Galatians 2 by looking, once again, at the timeline of events given by Paul in chapter one, including information found in Acts 9. Making a timeline for Paul's early ministry is difficult because different information is given in different places, some of it being very sketchy. Imagine if someone were trying to piece together the story of your life based on things you wrote to other people. To one person you might have given a very detailed account, to another you might have omitted something that appeared to be very significant in the first letter. It could be very confusing—as it is in Paul's case! So we will just do our best with the information we have.

- Paul persecutes the church—Gal. 1:13
- Paul advances in Judaism—Gal. 1:14
- Paul meets Christ and is called to preach to the Gentiles—Gal. 1:15-16
- Paul stays in Damascus for a few days, preaching there—Acts 9:19-20
- Paul goes to Arabia, then back to Damascus—Gal. 1:17
- Paul preaches in Damascus until there is a plot on his life—Acts 9:22-25
- Paul goes to Jerusalem three years later for 15 days, meets Peter and James—Gal. 1:18-19; Acts 9:26-28
- Paul's life is threatened in Jerusalem, he's taken to Caesarea and sent on to Tarsus—Acts 9:29-30
- Paul goes to Syria and Cilicia—Gal. 1:21
- Paul is unknown by sight to the churches in Judea—Gal. 1:22
- Paul's reputation as a preacher of the faith is known and God is glorified because of it—Gal. 1:23-24

In our study today, Paul continues to give his credentials, as it were, to being a true apostle with the true gospel message—chosen by God, taught by Jesus, approved by the apostles, and validated by his confrontation with Peter.

Day 1

Daily Facts

Read Galatians 2:1-5

1. What happened 14 years later? v. 1

   ✢ Why did he go there? v. 2a

This was a very important moment in the history of the church. It was a divine appointment! Although there is some confusion on the matter, most scholars believe it was at this time—on this particular trip to Jerusalem—that the famous Jerusalem Council was held. This would be a turning point in Paul's cause, as it was at this council that the decision was made that Gentile believers did not need to submit to Jewish laws. Because the rest of this passage can be difficult, you may find the New Living Translation easier to understand.

2. In verse 2, we see that there was a meeting set up. From this verse:

   ✢ Whom did Paul meet with at this time? Whom do you think this refers to?

   ✢ What information did he share with them?

   ✢ In what manner did he meet with them? Why did he say he did it this way? See if you can explain what he was thinking here.

Titus was an important element in this equation. He would be the test case! If the apostles agreed with Paul, they wouldn't require this Gentile believer to be circumcised.

3. Was Titus compelled to be circumcised? v. 3

   ✢ How did this confirm the heart of Paul's message—that salvation is by grace alone?

- Paul says that there were some there who had come in by stealth to spy out their liberty in order to bring them into bondage (verse 4). If salvation is by grace alone, why would it have been bondage for Titus to submit to circumcision?

- If Paul and Titus (and the apostles) had submitted to the pressure of the false brethren, what would have happened to the gospel message? v. 5

Making it Personal

Besides Paul, there are two important people in our passage today—Titus and Barnabas. As already noted, the presence of Titus was important to Paul for the situation at hand. Barnabas was simply important to Paul.

His help extended back to the early days of Paul's ministry, when he introduced Paul to Peter and James on that first trip to Jerusalem (Acts 9:26-27). In Acts 11:19-26, another discovery is made when we read that Barnabas left his thriving ministry in Antioch to search for Paul in Tarsus in order to bring him back to help. Barnabas saw Paul's value and extended his hand toward him. In Paul's case, Barnabas truly fulfilled the meaning of his name, which was "Son of Encouragement."

4. As you consider what Barnabas was to Paul, can you think of anyone who would consider you his or her "Barnabas"? In what ways are you ministering to him or her?

We know that Barnabas and Paul ministered together on the first missionary journey (Acts 13:2-4), but before they could leave on their second trip, they separated (Acts 15:36-40). Although we hear no more of Barnabas, Paul goes on to be the greatest missionary of all time.

- Consider how you would feel if the one you were helping ended up being used in a greater way than you. Can you submit to this thought? If you can (and you might stop right now and pray over this!), it will free you up to give them the best of yourself, just like Barnabas did with Paul!

Digging Deeper

- *Circumcision* was the key element in the struggle between law and grace. Using a Concordance or a Bible dictionary, do a simple study on the importance of this covenant to the Jews. See if you can discover why it was such an important issue in the early church. For help you may start with Genesis 17:1-14.

- Do your best to summarize today's passage in a couple of sentences.

Stone of Remembrance: "By the works of the law no flesh shall be justified." Galatians 2:16b

Day 2

Daily Facts

Read Galatians 2:6-10

In verse 2, Paul said that he shared with the apostles exactly what he was saying in his message to the Gentiles, in order to see if they were in agreement.

1. From what we have studied so far, what would have been the main thrust of that message?

- How did Titus—the test case—prove that the apostles agreed with Paul's message?

2. According to verse 6, did the apostles add anything to Paul's message?

This goes back to the intent of these first two chapters, emphasizing, again, that Paul's message was from Christ alone and that nothing (even now) had been given to him by the apostles. When Paul shared with the apostles the content of what he was preaching, there must have been great rejoicing as they realized that they were indeed preaching the same gospel message!

- What was recognized at this meeting? vv. 7-8

- What did the "pillars" of the church do for Paul and Barnabas at this time? v. 9

- As they were sent out to continue their ministry to the Gentiles, what was the only thing the apostles asked of them? v. 10

The apostles were referring here to the poor believers in Jerusalem, whom Paul was more than eager to help.

3. Although Paul's ministry was to the Gentiles, Romans 15 reveals the reason why he was so eager to help the saints in Jerusalem. How does he see the situation? Romans 15:25-27

Making it Personal

Paul makes the point in this letter that he is no respecter of persons. In Galatians 1:10, he stated that he was not a people pleaser but a servant of Christ. In our passage today, he mentions those of high reputation (those who seemed to be something) and says that what they were made no difference to him, because God shows no partiality.

4. Are you a people pleaser or can you say with Paul that you are simply a servant of Christ? How can you know for sure? Let Paul's own statements be your guide:

   - Are you seeking the favor of men? Gal. 1:10 NASB (Who's favor do you seek—man's or God's?)

   - Are you striving to please men? Gal. 1:10 NASB (Do you put yourself on your best behavior when someone of "reputation" comes into your midst?)

   - Does it make any difference to you if a person is of high reputation? Gal. 2:6 NASB (Are you more apt to do something sacrificial for someone you think can make a difference for you?)

   - How did you do? (These are areas we all struggle in!) What areas do you need to pray about/work on?

Digging Deeper

- Acts 15:1-20 gives us the account of the important meeting known as the Jerusalem Council. This is important to our understanding of the letter to the Galatians. Read the account and answer these questions: What prompted it? Who were the major players? What was the important point? What was the decision?

- Do your best to summarize today's passage in a couple of sentences.

- Review your memory verse.

Day 3

Daily Facts

Read Galatians 2:11-13

In today's passage, Paul recounts an event that will make a solid point to the Galatians about the practical application of the gospel of grace, as well as confirm and validate his position as apostle.

1. Look back at Acts 11:19-26 and see, again, what was happening in Antioch.

   - Who came to Antioch? Galatians 2:11

   - How did Paul react to him during his time there?

2. Paul says that Peter stood condemned (NASB). Verse 12 explains why. Explain what Peter did by answering the following questions:

(Note—The term "certain men from James" refers to Judaizers who probably claimed to have been sent by James.)

   - What had Peter done in the past—before the Judaizers came to Antioch?

   - What did he do after they came?

✣ What does Paul say was Peter's motive for this change in his behavior?

Consider the fact that the church in Antioch was made up predominantly of Gentile believers. The great apostle Peter was there with them. He ate with them. He recognized and appreciated them as fellow Christians. Then, when certain Jews claiming to be sent by James came to town (men who claimed to be believers but who separated themselves from the Gentile Christians), Peter separated himself from them too.

3. Peter's example was so compelling. What was the immediate result of his actions? v. 13

✣ See if you can explain what this would have done to the thinking process of the Gentiles in Antioch. (What kind of a message would this have sent them? What kind of confusion would it have brought?)

✣ Do you understand why, in this situation, it was urgent that Paul take a stand (verse 11)? Share your thoughts.

Making it Personal

We can only imagine Peter's embarrassment when Paul stood in opposition to his hypocrisy. He had succumbed to the pressure of people pleasing. Then Barnabas and the others played follow-the-leader. Haven't we been guilty of these same things?

4. How able are you to follow the convictions of your own heart? When you see others going a certain way, but your conviction is otherwise, are you able to stand your ground and do what you believe God's will to be—or do you cave?

- From the example given in our passage today, why is it important for you to follow the conviction in your heart as to the truth of the Word rather than seeking to fall in line with other people?

Digging Deeper

We learned yesterday that Peter was instrumental in the Jerusalem Council's final decision (not to put Gentile converts under the law). That was because God had already spoken to Peter on this point. Peter knew the truth! His doctrine wasn't wrong—his actions were.

- Using Acts 10:9-16, give the account of God's revelation to Peter on this point. Look ahead to verses 34-35 for Peter's statement as to what he learned from this experience.

- Do your best to summarize today's passage in a couple of sentences.

- Review your memory verse.

Day 4

Daily Facts

Read Galatians 2:14-21

Paul now begins to lay the foundation for the doctrinal point he is making in this letter. It appears as if the rest of this chapter consists of his confrontational dialogue with Peter.

1. Peter knew the truth, and he had previously acted according to it—living, in essence, like a Gentile. What was he now, by his actions, trying to make the Gentiles do? v. 14

- ✣ What had both Peter and Paul learned about salvation, according to verse 16?

Verse 16 is a very important verse, because it is the first time in this letter, and perhaps in any of his letters, that Paul communicated his great message of justification by faith. Because his ministry was to the Gentiles, Paul is the one who grasped this doctrine while it seems everyone else was still trying to get a handle on it.

2. Look up the word "justified." If possible, use a Bible dictionary. What does it mean?

- ✣ See if you can explain what Paul means when he says that all men—Jews and Gentiles alike—are saved by faith. (The majority of the rest of this letter will be a further examination of this concept.)

In the Greek, the word for justified is *dikaioo*, which means to declare righteous. Some antonyms for this word are: to judge, to find fault with, and to condemn. Verse 16 says that a man is not justified (or declared righteous) by the works of the law but by faith. In fact, Paul goes on to say here "for by the works of the law no flesh shall be justified"! Is that news to you?

3. What happens if, while seeking to be justified by faith in Christ, we put ourselves back under the law? vv. 17-18

- ✣ Have you ever thought of "working for your salvation" as a sin? What does it mean to you to work for your salvation?

Paul says that *through the law he died to the law that he might live to God.* He then goes on to make one of his most incredible statements, describing his position "in Christ."

4. Using Paul's exact words in verse 20, what is your position in regard to Christ's crucifixion? v. 20a (Make it personal.)

   - Who lives now—you or Christ?

   - Describe your life now as you live it in the flesh.

5. What is Paul's final and dramatic statement on the subject? v. 21b

Making it Personal

6. Just how amazing do you find it that your justification before God (your right standing with God) is by faith and not by works?

   - Are you making yourself a transgressor by placing yourself back under the law? If so, what do you think you should do about this?

Digging Deeper

- Go back through our study this week and see how many examples we have of the great courage of Paul. Where do you think we would be today if he hadn't been willing to take a stand?

- Do your best to summarize today's passage in a couple of sentences.

- Review your memory verse.

Day 5

Overview of Galatians 2

Today we will be looking at the passage we have studied this week as a whole. The goal is to find the main lessons the Lord has for us from this chapter. Don't worry about being clever or profound—just do your best!

Find the Facts …

1. See if you can state the *content* of this week's passage in a couple of sentences. You can use your daily summary statements to help you come up with one main theme or summary of the chapter. (Who is speaking, what is taking place, what is the main subject?)

Look for the Heart …

2. What do you think is the main *lesson* of this chapter? (What spiritual truths are taught here? Look for a command, a word of exhortation, a promise, etc.)

Hear Him Speak …

3. Look for a *personal application* from the content of this chapter. It should come from the lesson you got from the chapter (question 2). How will you apply the lesson to yourself?

4. Was there a particular verse that ministered to you this week? What was it and how did it minister to you?

5. Write out your stone of remembrance *from memory*!

LESSON THREE
Galatians 3

Oh, those foolish Galatians. Having begun in the Spirit, were they now trying to be perfected in the flesh? Salvation by faith, yes, but growing up in Christ—doesn't that only come through hard work, living according to the rules, and striving to please God?

You say that you are also in this trap? Who has beguiled you? Who has tricked you into thinking this way? It's not the Spirit of God. It's not the Word of God. Then who is it?

Day 1
Daily Facts

Read Galatians 3:1-5

1. What had Paul so clearly portrayed to the Galatians that it was as if they had been there themselves? v. 1

We almost get the impression here that Paul had witnessed this scene himself. Isn't it possible that he did? Have you ever thought of him there, witnessing the crucifixion?

2. After reminding them of this most significant event in history, what question did he ask them? v. 2

   - This was a rhetorical question. The answer was implied in the question. They weren't Jews and hadn't lived under the law—so how had they received the Spirit?

   - How does Romans 10:17 agree with this assessment?

3. What was Paul's next question? v. 3

- Considering what you know about the situation, what is Paul actually saying to them in verse 3? Try using your own words.

4. A final question, along the same lines—did God give them His Spirit and work miracles among them because of what they *did* or simply because they *believed* what they heard when Paul shared the good news with them? (v. 5)

- How does Romans 10:9-10 show how this takes place?

Making it Personal

Consider these questions Paul asked the Galatians in regard to your own faith and spiritual growth:

- Did you receive the Spirit by the works of the law or by the hearing of faith?
- Having begun in the Spirit, are you now being made perfect by the flesh?

This is personal! It makes all the difference!

- You were saved by faith—now how are you going to live?
- You were saved by faith—now how will you grow in spiritual maturity?
- You were saved by faith—now how will you minister?

5. Share your personal thoughts on this matter. Dig deep!

Digging Deeper

✣ In verse 4 Paul says, *"Did you suffer so many things in vain—if indeed it was in vain?"* If the Galatians submitted themselves to the law, after all God had done for them through grace, many things would have been in vain. Share why each of the following would have been in vain for the Galatians:

- ✓ *Christ's death*—(you may see Galatians 2:21)

- ✓ *Paul's work and suffering*—(consider his work among these very people in Acts 14:1-20)

- ✓ *Their own suffering* (consider the difficulty of Christianity in those early days—Paul is our example)

✣ Do your best to summarize today's passage in a couple of sentences.

Stone of Remembrance: "The just shall live by faith." Galatians 3:11

Day 2

Daily Facts

Read Galatians 3:6-14

1. How did Abraham acquire his right standing with God, according to verse 6?

- ✢ Abraham has physical descendants (the Jews) and spiritual descendants. How do you become a spiritual descendant of Abraham? v. 7

There are a couple of interesting and significant things here. First, Abraham wasn't a Jew. There were no Jewish people before Abraham. He was the father of the nation of Israel—that nation was born out of him by way of the promise of God. Second, the law hadn't yet been given at the time Abraham was declared righteous. And even the covenant of circumcision wasn't a part of the plan until after Abraham believed.

2. How did God declare his love and intended blessings upon all people—Jew and Gentile alike—in his original promise to Abraham? v. 8

- ✢ How does our faith bring us into this promised blessing? v. 9

- ✢ Why would this point undo the Judaizers claim to having something (the law) over the Gentiles?

3. Explain why it is actually a curse to be under the law. v. 10

- ✢ If the law brings a curse—can it also bring justification? Share what you remember from last week's study about the word justification.

- ✢ How are we to live? v. 11

This is not a New Testament idea—Paul is quoting from Habakkuk 2:4.

- ✢ Is "the law" of faith? (v. 12) What does *"he who practices them shall live by them"* mean? Can you live by both the law and faith? What must you do?

4. What did Christ do for us and how did He do it? v. 13

- How did this fulfill the promise to Abraham on our behalf? v. 14

- How do we receive the promise of the Spirit?

Making it Personal

5. How do you know *by personal experience* that it's a curse to live under the law?

    - Is this living? What kind of life did Jesus promise us? See John 10:10b

    - In a word, what is it the just shall *do* by faith? v. 11

This is the word that brought freedom to Martin Luther. As he was reading these very words (in Romans 1:17) he saw the word *live* and realized that he wasn't living. He was struggling. He was suffering. This verse opened his eyes to the truth! The just shall *live* by faith!

- Is there freedom in this thought for you?

Digging Deeper

- Take heart to the meaning of Romans 8:2-6, as you consider it verse by verse:

  verse 2

  verse 3

verse 4

verse 5

verse 6

✢ Do your best to summarize today's passage in a couple of sentences.

✢ Review your memory verse.

Day 3

Daily Facts

Read Galatians 3:15-22

Warren Wiersbe (*The Bible Exposition Commentary, Volume 1*) says that Paul uses six arguments in chapters 3 and 4 to prove the point that God saves sinners through faith not works. We have already looked at two of them in the first 14 verses—a personal argument (based on their own personal experience) and a Scriptural argument (where Paul quoted six Old Testament Scriptures to prove his point). The next argument Paul uses is one of logic. We will see that in our passage today. We might entitle today's passage, "The Law or the Promise."

1. Paul begins by using the example of a human covenant or agreement—it could be a will. From verse 15, once this document has been ratified, or agreed upon, what is the case?

✢ If this is the case with a human covenant—what would we expect concerning a covenant made by God?

Paul is referring to the covenant God made with Abraham. The original promise was given in Genesis 12:3: "All the nations shall be blessed in you." In Genesis 15, God spoke to Abraham again. It was at this time that the covenant was sealed.

2. To whom were the promises made? v. 16

- In relation to the promise, when did the law come? v. 17

- What should this fact have made them see?

- Was the inheritance based on the law or on the promise? v. 18

The Judaizers, taking their stand on the supremacy of the law, were insinuating that the law invalidated the promise. Paul says the promise came first. That would be the covenant that would take supremacy.

3. So the next obvious question would be, why the law then? What is the answer, according to these verses?

   verse 19

   verse 22

4. What would have been the only occasion for righteousness to be based on law? v. 21

Warren Wiersbe sums it up, "The law cannot change the promise, and the law is not greater than the promise, but the law is not contrary to the promise, they work together to bring sinners to the Savior."

John Calvin says it this way, "The [role] of the law is to show us the disease in such a way that it shows no hope of cure; whereas the [role] of the gospel is to bring a remedy to those who are past hope."

Making it Personal

5. How did the law bring *you* to the Savior?

Digging Deeper

- God spoke His promises to Abraham on several occasions through the years. These promises were fulfilled in Christ, and you are included in this heritage! Share the specific promises that were made on each occasion.

  Genesis 12:1-3, 7

  Genesis 15, 1-5, 18

  Genesis 17:1-8

  Genesis 22:16-18

- Do your best to summarize today's passage in a couple of sentences.

- Review your memory verse.

Day 4

Daily Facts

Read Galatians 3:23-29

Today we continue with the logical part of Paul's argument that faith in Christ is superior to obedience to the law. As Paul continues relating the law to the promise, he helps us to understand that the law was necessary, but not permanent.

1. Going back to what we learned in our passage yesterday, to whom were the *promises* made? v. 16

   - What is the significance of the fact that the word was *seed* and not seeds?

Though there was fulfillment of promises in Abraham's lifetime, the greatest promise was spiritual, to be fulfilled through his seed, Christ.

2. Read verses 23-25 and, in simple terms, answer the following questions:

   - Until Christ came, what was the law like?

   - What was its job?

   - What was its hopeful outcome?

   - After Jesus came to the earth and died on the cross for our sins, did we need the law any longer? What did we need?

The word for tutor, in these verses, speaks of a slave entrusted with the guidance of a child. This one would care for the child, discipline the child, conduct the child to and from school, teach the child manners, etc. As important as the job of this slave was, it was only temporary. Once the child became an adult, he no longer needed this tutor to show the way.

- With these thoughts in mind, explain the message of verses 23-25 in your own words.

3. How is it that we stand as sons and daughters of God?

- When we were baptized into Christ, what did we do? v. 27

The NASB says it this way, "For all of you who were baptized into Christ have clothed yourselves with Christ."

- If we are "clothed with Christ," what difference does that make to our standing in the world? v. 28

- Does this mean that if you are of Jewish heritage you are no longer a Jew, or if you are a female you now have no gender? What do you think it means?

Making it Personal

4. Share what it means to you personally to be *clothed with Christ.*

Digging Deeper

- There is nothing like the word *promise*. We love it, don't we? Verse 29 tells us that if we belong to Christ, then we are Abraham's offspring and *heirs according to promise.* Let's look at Ephesians 1:3-14 and see what some of the promises of our inheritance in Christ are. Write out as many as you find there (you will be blessed!).

- Do your best to summarize today's passage in a couple of sentences.

- Review your memory verse.

Day 5

Overview of Galatians 3

Today we will be looking at the passage we have studied this week as a whole. The goal is to find the main lessons the Lord has for us from this chapter. Don't worry about being clever or profound—just do your best!

Find the Facts ...

1. See if you can state the *content* of this week's passage in a couple of sentences. You can use your daily summary statements to help you come up with one main theme or summary of the chapter. (Who is speaking, what is taking place, what is the main subject?)

Look for the Heart ...

2. What do you think is the main *lesson* of this chapter? (What spiritual truths are taught here? Look for a command, a word of exhortation, a promise, etc.)

Hear Him Speak ...

3. Look for a *personal application* from the content of this chapter. It should come from the lesson you got from the chapter (question 2). How will you apply the lesson to yourself?

4. Was there a particular verse that ministered to you this week? What was it and how did it minister to you?

5. Write out your stone of remembrance *from memory*!

LESSON FOUR
Galatians 4

Galatians 4 picks up right where Galatians 3 ends. Paul continues to make the case that we who are saved are heirs of the promises made to Abraham, brought about through Christ. The main point in this section of his letter is the superiority of grace over the law. Why would anyone want to place themselves under the law when the grace of God has saved them? That's Paul's question! He continues to ask it in our passage today.

Day 1
Daily Facts

Read Galatians 4:1-7

1. What does verse 1 tell us about the heir to an estate who is still a child?

    ✢ What is his daily situation according to verse 2?

This child would not actually be a slave—he would be an heir. But as a child, his daily life would be directed and guided by others. Though owner of everything, he would not have the right of ownership until the date set by his father.

In Jewish culture, we know that a child becomes an adult at the age of 12. In Roman culture, the father was the one who would determine the time for this coming of age. Until that date, the child was held in bondage, so to speak.

✢ Before faith in Christ (while we were yet children) what was the situation for us? v. 3

This verse could be speaking of being held in bondage to the Mosaic law or to any other religious practice in which Paul's readers found themselves before Christ. The point has to do with bondage.

- ✣ Look carefully at verse 3—*who* was held in bondage to the elemental things of the world? (What pronoun does Paul use?) How does this apply to you?

2. What happened that changed the situation for those in bondage? v. 4

Just like the Roman father who determined when the time was right for his son to become an adult, God the Father had a predetermined time when He would send His Son Jesus to the earth to fulfill that which had been promised to Abraham.

- ✣ What was God's purpose in doing this? v. 5

God's purpose was to make slaves into sons. One of the meanings of the word *redeem* is to remove from the marketplace (speaking of a slave market). God sent His Son in order to redeem those who were slaves to the law—to buy them right out of the slave market!

3. What is the proof that we are no longer slaves, but sons? v. 6

- ✣ What is the final outcome of our passage today, according to verse 7?

Making it Personal

Today you may feel like a son or a daughter. You may be singing out "Abba! Father!" in your heart right now. Or maybe today you feel more like a slave. Maybe today you are struggling with guilt and with doubt. You know what? Your feelings have nothing to do with it. The question is, did you listen to the message of truth and believe? If you did, then you can know that you are a child of God.

4. Let Ephesians 1:13-14 speak the words of truth that overrule your feelings. What does it tell you in these verses? (Make it personal.)

Digging Deeper

- Romans 8:14-17 agrees perfectly with Paul's final thoughts in our passage today. Read these verses, then answer the following questions from v. 15:

  - ✓ From what spirit are we released when we receive God's Spirit?

  - ✓ From what we have learned so far, had the Galatians been released from this spirit? Why or why not.

  - ✓ Have you been released from this spirit? (If the answer is no, does today's *"Making it Personal" section* help you?)

- Do your best to summarize today's passage in a couple of sentences.

Stone of Remembrance: "Christ has redeemed us from the curse of the law ..." Galatians 3:13a

Day 2

Daily Facts

Read Galatians 4:8-11

Galatians 4:1-7 is permeated with the idea of slavery. Verse 1 speaks of heirs who are children being no better off than slaves. Verse 3 says, "And that's the way it was for us before Christ came. We were slaves to the spiritual powers of this world." Verse 5, speaking of Jesus says, "God sent Him to buy freedom for us who were slaves to the law." And verse 7 says, "Now you are no longer a slave, but God's own child." (All quotes from the NLT.) This concept of slavery continues in our passage today.

1. How does verse 8 define what we were slaves to before faith in Christ?

The NLT translates this verse, "Before you Gentiles knew God, you were slaves to so-called gods that do not even exist." This would be referring to idol worship.

- What kind of slavery is specified in verse 9?

- How did this slavery manifest itself? v. 10

The worthless and elemental things (NASB), to which Paul referred, were rituals, festivals, and celebrations that were a part of the Jewish calendar, according to the law. Perhaps a Jewish Christian might still participate in these occasions because they were part of his heritage, but why would a Gentile feel the need to do so? Unless he felt it would merit some special favor of God or fulfill some sort of duty.

2. Paul pointed to this same thing in his letter to the Colossians. How does Paul strongly exhort them to freedom from the rules and rituals of Judaism? Colossians 2:16

- Why was it not necessary for them to keep these kinds of rules and observances? Colossians 2:17 (See if you can explain what this means.)

Making it Personal

3. Do you do any particular thing, participate in any particular activity, or even eat or drink in a certain way *because you think you will earn God's favor*? Spend some time on this thought and share what you discover.

- Do you judge anyone else according to these types of stipulations? If you find you have been doing this, won't you lay this type of judgment down right now, confess it as sin, and let others find their own freedom in Christ?

Digging Deeper

- Colossians 2 gives us one of the clearest pictures of the fullness or completeness of our redemption from sin. Read verses 13-15 and answer these questions:

What <u>was</u> our condition? v. 13

What did Christ do for us? vv. 13-14

What did He do to the rulers and authorities? v. 15 (We might think of these "rulers and authorities" as the powers behind the "so-called gods that do not even exist" of Galatians 4:8.)

Why Paul can now say, " Therefore, let no one judge you" (verse 16)?

- Do your best to summarize today's passage in a couple of sentences.

- Review your memory verse.

Day 3

Daily Facts

Read Galatians 4:12-20

Now Paul gets personal. In his outline of six arguments, Warren Wiersbe calls this one the *sentimental argument*. Paul takes a turn from the logical and historical arguments in favor of the concept of grace, and he makes a plea with his heart.

1. Paul begins by urging (*begging*—NASB) them to become as he is, since he has become as they are. What do you think he is saying here? v. 12

2. What was the situation when Paul first preached to them? v. 13

   - How did they receive him? v. 14

   - How extensive was their love for him then? v. 15

No one knows for sure what Paul's problem was at the time, but many take this passage to indicate that it was a problem with his eyes. What the exact problem was isn't really the point. The point is that the Galatians loved Paul.

Paul says in verse 15 (NASB), "Where then is the sense of blessing you had?" In other words, what happened to the way you felt about me then?

- What is Paul thinking has happened? v. 16

3. In verse 17, Paul refers to the Judaizers who are hounding the Galatians. How does Paul say they are seeking them, and what does he think is their motive?

- From what did they want to exclude the Galatians?

4. What was Paul's personal agony over the Galatians like at this time? v. 19

Paul had already labored for their birth in Christ. They had already been through that process. But Paul was now going through it all over again, so that Christ could truly be formed in them. What a thought!

- What was Paul's desire? v. 20

- Why would it have been easier for Paul to speak to them face to face?

Making it Personal

How sad that Paul had to ask the question, "Have I therefore become your enemy because I tell you the truth?" (verse 16). Sometimes telling the truth makes enemies—but we still need to tell the truth.

5. How does Ephesians 4:15 direct you in this oftentimes difficult process?

   - How does Galatians 6:1 give you perspective on how to do this?

   - Is there someone to whom you need to *"speak the truth in love"* today?

Digging Deeper

- 2 Corinthians 12 tells about Paul's experience with a thorn in the flesh. Many think he was referring to this very thorn in Galatians 4. Read the account in 2 Corinthians 12:1-10 and share: 1) What was the occasion of Paul receiving this thorn? 2) What was God's instruction to him about it? 3) What was Paul's reaction to this word of God? 4) What encouragement does this passage bring to you?

- Do your best to summarize today's passage in a couple of sentences.

- Review your memory verse.

Day 4

Daily Facts

Read Galatians 4:21-31

Paul now moves on to an allegorical argument, looking back to Abraham again, only this time concentrating on the two women in Abraham's life—Sarah and Hagar. An allegory is a literary technique that presents a moral principle or truth by means of a fictional character and/or event. In this case, the story Paul uses is a true one—but he uses allegory to bring out a deeper spiritual meaning.

Paul begins, almost sarcastically, "Tell me, you who desire to be under the law, do you not hear the law?" That is a good question for these Galatians! Paul uses that beginning to go forth to teach them a truth that they would not have known.

The characters in this allegory are: Abraham, Sarah, Hagar, Ishmael, and Isaac. The events are the birth of two sons. The places Paul uses symbolically are Mount Sinai and the present Jerusalem (representing the Old Covenant of law) and the heavenly Jerusalem (representing the New Covenant of grace). The truth Paul wants to set forth has to do with slavery and freedom, the law and the promise.

1. In what manner were Abraham's two sons born? v. 22

    - How was the son of the bondwoman born? v. 23

    - How was the son of the free woman born?

    - Do you remember the promise from an earlier study on this subject? For help look at Genesis 15:4-5.

2 How does Paul describe Hagar in verse 24?

    - What two places correspond with Hagar and what does Hagar represent? v. 25

- From these thoughts, what covenant does Hagar stand for?

- Take a moment and read Genesis 16:1-4, 15-16 for an understanding of Hagar's story—this will be part of our *Digging Deeper* for today. Try to find out who she was, how she entered into Abraham's story, and what happened to her.

3. Without telling the story, Paul refers to the birth of Isaac by Sarah. Read Genesis 21:1-3 and make note as you read: what God did for Sarah, what Abraham's condition was, and when exactly Isaac was born.

   - What place does Sarah represent? Galatians 4:26

Hagar was a slave. Sarah was free. The birth of Ishmael was according to works (Sarah was trying to help God out); the birth of Isaac was all grace (both Sarah and Abraham were past the age of child bearing. He was a miracle, given according to the promise).

4. What does Paul say about us? vv. 28, 31

   - Why would he deduce this? Think back to what we have already learned about the promise.

5. What happened between the child born according to the flesh and the one born according to the Spirit? v. 29 (You can read the historical account in Genesis 21:8-12.)

   - What was the result of this problem? v. 30

Making it Personal

Just as there was a war between the flesh and the Spirit in the story of Ishmael and Isaac, so there will be a war in each of us when we choose to live by the Spirit rather than by the flesh. Our flesh doesn't want to let go! And there is a royal battle at every turn as we try to live this life of grace.

The Galatians were waging the battle right then! Their flesh was trying to keep hold of them, while Paul was giving his all to exhort them to live in the spirit of freedom. The difficult answer to Abraham was to cast out the bondwoman and her son. For the Galatians to follow that advice would mean to cast out the Judaizers who were causing them to listen to the flesh. But, what does it mean to us?

6. Considering your fight with legalism, works, and the flesh, what does it mean to you to *cast out the bondwoman and her son*? (Is there a ritual you need to let go of, a truth you need to take hold of, do you need to learn something, or might it be that you need to *unlearn* something?)

Digging Deeper

- Do your best to summarize today's passage in a couple of sentences.

- Review your memory verse.

Day 5

Overview of Galatians 4

Today we will be looking at the passage we have studied this week as a whole. The goal is to find the main lessons the Lord has for us from this chapter. Don't worry about being clever or profound—just do your best!

Find the Facts ...

1. See if you can state the *content* of this week's passage in a couple of sentences. You can use your daily summary statements to help you come up with one main theme or summary of the chapter. (Who is speaking, what is taking place, what is the main subject?)

Look for the Heart ...

2. What do you think is the main *lesson* of this chapter? (What spiritual truths are taught here? Look for a command, a word of exhortation, a promise, etc.)

Hear Him Speak ...

3. Look for a *personal application* from the content of this chapter. It should come from the lesson you got from the chapter (question 2). How will you apply the lesson to yourself?

4. Was there a particular verse that ministered to you this week? What was it and how did it minister to you?

5. Write out your stone of remembrance *from memory*!

LESSON FIVE
Galatians 5

Chapter 5 is a turning point in the letter to the Galatians. What began in chapter 1 as a theological explanation or an apologetic on the doctrine of grace will now begin to be practical. Verses 1-12 finish up Paul's argument for the superiority of grace over the law and then, from verse 13 through the end of the letter, Paul gets personal.

Day 1
Daily Facts

Read Galatians 5:1-4

Chapter 5 begins with the key verse or, we could say, the decisive statement of the entire letter to the Galatians!

1. What is the statement, as given in verse 1a? (NASB or NIV will give you the best understanding.)

   ⚜ How might you consider this a promise that you can claim?

2. Paul gives two words of exhortation in verse 1. What are they?

   ⚜

   ⚜

3. In verse 2, Paul says that if they receive circumcision, Christ will be of no profit to them. To whom is Paul speaking—those who are already circumcised or those who are considering it? What exactly is his message to them?

- ✠ Using verses 3 and 4, explain what Paul is trying to tell them.

  verse 3

  verse 4

Making it Personal

4. Looking back at the life-changing message of Galatians 5:1, what does it mean to you to be free (at liberty)?

   - ✓ Are you free? If not, identify, if you can, what is keeping you from the freedom Christ died to purchase for you.

   - ✓ Reclaim your freedom by laying down the burden you have picked up—this may be a time of confession and repentance, or simply an acknowledgment that you have been thinking wrong.

   - ✓ Now turn from the error of your ways/thinking by determining to follow Paul's exhortation in this verse.

Digging Deeper

There has been much controversy over verse 4 of this chapter. Some have taken it to mean that true believers can fall from God's saving grace—or, in other words, can lose their salvation. Of course, that was not Paul's meaning at all. In reading any portion of Scripture, we must take it in context with the rest of the Bible.

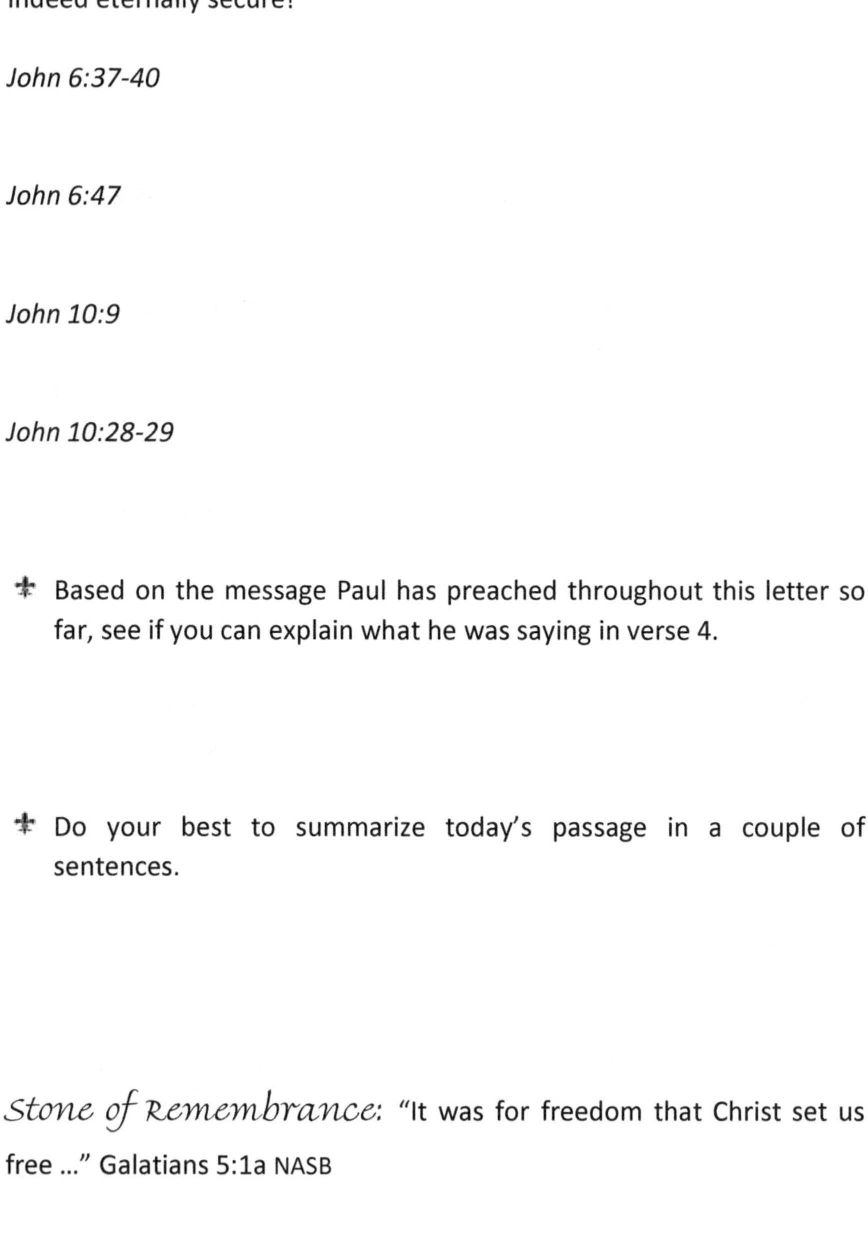

We will take this opportunity to look at what the Gospel of John teaches on the eternal security of the true believer. Share the message from each of these passages/verses and rejoice in the fact that you are indeed eternally secure!

John 6:37-40

John 6:47

John 10:9

John 10:28-29

- Based on the message Paul has preached throughout this letter so far, see if you can explain what he was saying in verse 4.

- Do your best to summarize today's passage in a couple of sentences.

Stone of Remembrance: "It was for freedom that Christ set us free ..." Galatians 5:1a NASB

Day 2

Daily Facts

Read Galatians 5:5-12

As Paul finishes up his doctrinal plea, he gets strong—in fact we could say he gets angry.

1. In our flesh, as we attempt to keep the law, are we found to be righteous? What is actually the case? v. 5

Legalists are hoping that by obeying the law they will become righteous. That will never happen. As Paul already pointed out—if they try to find righteousness through the keeping of one law, they will be under obligation to keep the whole law. And we all know that cannot be done.

- In Philippians 3:9, Paul shares his own heart on the matter. What is his hope, according to this verse?

- In what simple manner does Galatians 5:6 help us to understand that our righteousness is based on faith and not on keeping the law?

2. How were the Galatians doing before the coming of the "troublemakers"? v. 7a

- What had they been hindered from doing, according to this verse?

- Paul makes it clear who had *not* hindered them (verse 8). From your study of Galatians so far, who does he suggest *had* hindered them?

This is where we see Paul's anger escalate. God didn't hinder them from obeying the truth—and we can see from verse 12 that Paul has no pity on those who did!

3. Why was the problem so huge in Paul's eyes? v. 9

   - Explain what this means in regard to legalism and a local church. (Use an experience of your own, if you have one.)

   - What does Paul hopefully expect? v. 10

Making it Personal

Take a few moments to meditate on Philippians 3:9.

4. In whom have you been trying to be "found"... *yourself*—your righteousness, based on keeping the law, or *Christ*—and the righteousness that comes through faith in Him? Share your thoughts.

   - Paul said he wanted to be *found in Christ* and that the righteousness he wanted was *the righteousness that comes through faith in Christ*. You can't have it both ways. Which way do you choose?

Digging Deeper

- In verse 11, Paul makes the point that if he were preaching the need for circumcision in order to be saved, he would not be facing the persecution he faced and the *stumbling block of the cross* (NASB) would be abolished. See if you can explain why the cross is a stumbling block to those who want to work their way to heaven. See 1 Corinthians 1:20-24.

- Do your best to summarize today's passage in a couple of sentences.

- Review your memory verse.

Day 3

Daily Facts

Read Galatians 5:13-21

1. In verse 13, Paul brings us back to the original thought of freedom (liberty). We have been called to freedom! What are we *not* to do with our freedom? What does Paul mean here? (What might a person who is free from the law do?)

    - What *are* we to do with our freedom? v. 13b

Although Paul has been waging a war against legalism throughout this entire letter, he now shifts his emphasis and gives us a proper perspective on the law. The law cannot *save* us, but serving others in love ultimately fulfills the law in a way that our slavery to it cannot.

- How is the entire law summed up and fulfilled, according to verse 14?

In his commentary on Galatians, John Courson says, "Love is the one word that encapsulates the entire law. Not legalism—love."

- What was legalism causing the Galatians to do to one another? v. 15 What would be the result?

2. Paul now turns the tables and gives the antidote to the problem. What is his prescription? v. 16

   ✢ In simple terms, what do you think it means to walk in the Spirit?

3. Paul says that if we walk in the Spirit, we will not carry out the *lusts* of the flesh. He then goes on to give us a list of the *works* of the flesh (v. 19-21). List them here by category:

   Sexual sins—

   Religious sins—

   Interpersonal relationship sins—

4. What warning does Paul give to the one who *practices* such things? v. 21b

   ✢ Although we cannot know the spiritual state of another individual for certain, what is Paul deducing when he makes this statement?

Making it Personal

How was legalism causing the Galatians to bite and devour one another? We might think in today's terms: What Bible do you read? What devotional do you read? When you do read your Bible each day? How many chapters do you read? How long do you pray? What words do you use when you pray? What church do you go to? Do you sing hymns or do you sing praise songs? How much or how often do you tithe? And so on ...

5. Describe how these kinds of legalistic questions can cause Christians to bite and devour one another. Thinking in these terms—what does walking in the Spirit mean *personally* to you?

Digging Deeper

- Paul has told us in this section that the law is fulfilled in the statement, "You shall love your neighbor as yourself" (verse 14). See if you can explain how loving your neighbor fulfills the law that circumcision can never fulfill. You might see Matthew 23:23 for help.

- Do your best to summarize today's passage in a couple of sentences.

- Review your memory verse.

Day 4

Daily Facts

Read Galatians 5:22-26

1. Make a list of the characteristics that Paul calls the *fruit of the Spirit.* vv. 22-23

   - How are these characteristics produced, according to the name Paul has given them?

- Why do you think Paul calls them fruit rather than works?

- How can you have these characteristics produced in your own life?

2. We see in Galatians 5 that there are two forces at work—the Spirit and the flesh. How does verse 17 explain this?

   - But what is the truth about those who now belong to Christ? v. 24

   - How did Paul personalize this deep truth in Galatians 2:20?

   - Since we are now living the "crucified life" of faith, what is the answer for us, according to verse 25?

3. What final practical application does Paul make in verse 26?

   - See if you can tie his final exhortation here with their foundational problem of legalism.

Making it Personal

4. Which seems have the upper hand in your life today—the flesh or the Spirit?

   - If your answer is the flesh, verse 16 gives you the prescription to your problem. Apply this verse personally—what do you need to do and how might you begin doing it?

Digging Deeper

- Do your best to summarize today's passage in a couple of sentences.

- Review your memory verse.

Day 5

Overview of Galatians 5

Today we will be looking at the passage we have studied this week as a whole. The goal is to find the main lessons the Lord has for us from this chapter. Don't worry about being clever or profound—just do your best!

Find the Facts ...

1. See if you can state the *content* of this week's passage in a couple of sentences. You can use your daily summary statements to help you come up with one main theme or summary of the chapter. (Who is speaking, what is taking place, what is the main subject?)

Look for the Heart ...

2. What do you think is the main *lesson* of this chapter? (What spiritual truths are taught here? Look for a command, a word of exhortation, a promise, etc.)

Hear Him Speak ...

3. Look for a *personal application* from the content of this chapter. It should come from the lesson you got from the chapter (question 2). How will you apply the lesson to yourself?

4. Was there a particular verse that ministered to you this week? What was it and how did it minister to you?

5. Write out your stone of remembrance *from memory*!

LESSON SIX
Galatians 6

In chapters 5-6, Paul makes his transition from the doctrine of grace to the practice of grace. His final words in chapter 5 are an exhortation of how we *should not* be acting—boasting, challenging, envying one another (NASB)—as these are legalistic attitudes which damage the body of Christ. In chapter 6, he turns the tables from the negative to the positive by laying out the kinds of attitudes and actions we *should* be practicing—attitudes of grace that build up the body of Christ and are the fruit of a Spirit-filled life.

Day 1
Daily Facts

Read Galatians 6:1-5

Instead of boasting and challenging others—looking down on them as if we think we are better—Galatians 6:1 tells us how we *should* act toward one another. In fact, it gives us the formula for reacting to someone who is *overtaken in a trespass.*

1. To whom is Paul speaking in verse 1? From what we studied in our last lesson, to whom would he be referring in this verse? (*Is this you?*)

    - ✢ In a word, what is *always* to be the goal when it is discovered that a brother or sister has been overtaken by a sin? v. 1 (*Is that always your goal?*)

    - ✢ How do we want to do this, according to verse 1?

2. What do you think Paul means when he says we're to *consider ourselves lest we be tempted*?

   - Would a legalist naturally react to a person caught in sin according to Paul's exhortation in verse 1? How would they react?

   - How do *you* react to a faltering or even a failing Christian? Do you resemble the one who is spiritual or the legalist?

3. What do you think Paul means when he tells the Galatians to bear one another's burdens? v. 2

   - From what you know about the teachings of Christ, what "law of Christ" might he be referring to in verse 2?

   - How is Paul's exhortation to bear one another's burdens connected to his exhortation to gently restore the sinning Christian?

Making it Personal

4. There is such a push these days for us to have self-esteem and to think highly of ourselves. Paul doesn't see it that way. What do you think he means when he tells us that we deceive ourselves when we think we are something? v. 3

What Paul is doing in Galatians 6:3-5 is encouraging us to evaluate ourselves accurately, in light of Christ, taking care not to compare ourselves with others. The legalists were in the business of comparison. "If you do everything our way, then you are right." Paul says, "Never mind that!" In fact, it is probable that he is speaking to the legalist in verse 3 as the one who thinks he is something and deceives himself!

5. Taking from Paul's thoughts in Galatians 6:3-5 and Romans 12:3, share from a *personal perspective* the proper way to think about yourself.

   - Should you compare yourself with others? What happens to you when you do (share from personal experience)?

   - Instead of comparing, what are the things *you* can rejoice in? (Galatians 6: 4)

Digging Deeper

- Do your best to summarize today's passage in a couple of sentences.

Stone of Remembrance: "... God forbid that I should glory except in the cross of our Lord Jesus Christ ..." Galatians 6:14a

Day 2

Daily Facts

Read Galatians 6:6-10

In this chapter, Paul is talking about the kinds of attitudes and actions those who are spiritual should be practicing—attitudes and actions of grace.

1. What is another gracious act those who are spiritual should be practicing, according to verse 6?

   ✢ Consider the wording. Is this a suggestion or a command?

   ✢ What exactly is Paul saying here?

2. Paul moves from what might be considered a simple rule of etiquette to a very important rule of nature. What does he tell us about God in verse 7a?

   ✢ What does he tell us about the nature of sowing and reaping in this verse?

   ✢ How does he spiritualize this rule in verse 8?

3. Explain Paul's analogy using farming terms. What happens when a farmer plants a field of corn? What happens when he plants potatoes? Will he ever reap potatoes in the cornfield? Why?

   ✢ What kinds of things will the person who sows to the flesh reap? (You might look back at Galatians 5:19-23 for help.) Explain why this will be the case.

- In which field are you sowing—the field of the flesh or the field of the Spirit? Share some examples of how you are sowing to the Spirit in this life.

- If you are sowing to the Spirit, what can you expect *now* (see Galatians 5:22, 23)? What can you expect in the end (see Galatians 6:8)?

4. What word of encouragement does Paul give us in verse 9?

- What are we encouraged to do as a result? v. 10

Making it Personal

5. Are you growing weary of doing good? Have you been at it a long time but see little fruit from your labors? Share where you are at today.

- Can you take encouragement from Paul's words? Can you believe, based solely on the law of sowing and reaping, that in time you will be rewarded? Look at these verses that teach a similar message and be encouraged today!

  2 Chronicles 15:7

  Haggai 2:4-5

  1 Corinthians 15:58

- What does 1 Corinthians 9:24 teach us? Will you do it???

Digging Deeper

Paul's teaching in our passage today, on sowing to the Spirit, perfectly complements the teaching of Jesus in Matthew 6:19-21. Read the words that Jesus spoke in Matthew 6 and share what the heart of the message really is.

- Do your best to summarize today's passage in a couple of sentences.

- Review your memory verse.

Day 3

Daily Facts

Read Galatians 6:11-14

1. We come now to Paul's final words to the Galatians. How does he introduce this final thrust of his message? v. 11

Not only was Paul writing these final words with his own hand, but it is as if he is saying, "I'm writing this with large letters, so listen up!" He now turns from the practical back to the original reason for writing the letter, touching again on what he has already said.

2. What are the legalists trying to do to the Galatians? v. 12

Paul gives two reasons for this in verse 12: In order for them to make a good showing in the flesh, and in order for them not to suffer persecution. Both of these reasons come from the fact that the legalists were trying to have it both ways.

They wanted to be aligned with Christ—but as Jews. They didn't want to be judged by the Jews, they wanted to still be accepted by them. They, in essence, were using the Galatians for their own purposes.

✢ How does Paul say this in verse 13?

This isn't an easy passage to understand, but basically Paul is saying that although the legalists can't even keep the law themselves, they receive glory in fact that they can compel Gentile believers to come under the law in regard to circumcision. The NASB says it this way, "...They desire to have you circumcised, that they may boast in your flesh."

3. We see in verse 14 that Paul reacts strongly to the thought of these legalists boasting in another person's flesh! Although we might even think that Paul could boast in regard to bringing someone to Christ, what does Paul say is *the only thing* that he will boast in?

✢ How does he describe the work of the cross in his life? v. 14b

Making it Personal

In a word of personal testimony, George Mueller said it this way: "There was a day when I died, utterly died, died to George Mueller, his opinions, preferences, tastes, and will; died to the world, its approval or censure; died to the approval or blame of even my brethren and friends—since then I have studied only to show myself approved to God."

4. Is there an area in which you need to die today? Won't you ask the Lord for His help? Write out your prayer, being specific with the Lord about your area of need. Expect Him to help you there! (This is personal, not to be shared with your group.)

Digging Deeper

In his commentary, Warren Wiersbe says that Paul keeps coming back to the cross. What a neat thing to realize. It was the essence of everything to Paul. Look at these verses in Galatians in which Paul speaks of the center of history—the cross of Christ: 2:20-21; 3:13; 4:5; 5:11, 24; 6:12, 14. How important is the cross of Christ in *your* world?

- Do your best to summarize today's passage in a couple of sentences.

- Review your memory verse.

Day 4

Daily Facts

Read Galatians 6:15-18

1. Paul repeats himself in his final words to the Galatians (see Galatians 5:6). What important thing does he want them to know? v. 15

   - Do you understand Paul's point in this verse? If you are a new creation in Christ, does it matter what condition you were in when you came to Him?

   - How does Paul say this in 2 Corinthians 5:17?

   - What did he already say to the Galatians about this in Galatians 3:28?

   - Is there anything you can take *personally* from the thought that in Christ you are a new creation?

2. As he finishes up his letter, laying out the truth of salvation by grace through faith alone, what does Paul promise the one who walks by this rule? v. 16

3. What are Paul's final words to the Judaizers? v. 17

- How are Paul's final words to the Galatians loving and hopeful? v. 18

Making it Personal

Although we know from Scripture that Paul was circumcised, the marks he speaks of in verse 17 are different marks. The NASB calls them the brand-marks of Jesus. Paul is talking about scars. Dr. Samuel M. Zwemer says this about scars: "Scars are the authentic marks of faithful discipleship and true spiritual leadership ... Those are tests of sincerity that no one can challenge ..." Amy Carmichael has written a poem about scars. It ends with these words: "Can he have followed far who has no wound? No Scar?"

4. Do you bear in your body any *brand-marks* of Jesus? Do you have any scars? Have you followed closely enough to the Savior to share in His sufferings? Share your heart on these matters.

Digging Deeper

- Do your best to summarize today's passage in a couple of sentences.

- Review your memory verse.

Day 5

Overview of Galatians 6

Today we will be looking at the passage we have studied this week as whole. The goal is to find the main lessons the Lord has for us from this chapter. Don't worry about being clever or profound—just do your best!

Find the Facts ...

1. See if you can state the *content* of this week's passage in a couple of sentences. You can use your daily summary statements to help you come up with one main theme or summary of the chapter. (Who is speaking, what is taking place, what is the main subject?)

Look for the Heart ...

2. What do you think is the main *lesson* of this chapter? (What spiritual truths are taught here? Look for a command, a word of exhortation, a promise, etc.)

Hear Him Speak ...

3. Look for a *personal application* from the content of this chapter. It should come from the lesson you got from the chapter (question 2). How will you apply the lesson to yourself?

4. Was there a particular verse that ministered to you this week? What was it and how did it minister to you?

5. Write out your stone of remembrance *from memory*!

ABOUT THE AUTHOR

Linda has dedicated her life to serving the Lord as a teacher, writer, and speaker. While teaching the Word of God, training leaders, and speaking at retreats and other women's ministry functions, she has also written curriculum for over 20 books of the Bible.

If you would be interested in having more information about her ministry, please visit her blog at www.lindaoborne.wordpress.com, or email her at myutmost1@aol.com.

www.ingramcontent.com/pod-product-compliance
Lightning Source LLC
LaVergne TN
LVHW020656100826
845148LV00012B/2521

* 9 7 8 0 6 1 5 8 0 3 9 3 7 *